COMMUNICATION

Develop The Skills Required To Navigate Difficult
Conversations Using Effective Communication-listening

*(The Craft Of Successful Communication Unlocking
Professional)*

Tino-Erik Conrad

TABLE OF CONTENT

Introduction 1

Chapter 1: Easy Ways To Improve Relationship Communication 10

Chapter 2: Methods To A Resolution 14

Chapter 3: The Art Of Communicating Your Thoughts And Emotions Across Various Mediums. 21

Chapter 4: The Influence Of Self-Esteem 38

Chapter 5: Learn How To Good Value Your Children In Public. 44

Chapter 6: How To Enhance Your Conversational Iq 55

Chapter 7: How To Manage Anxiety And Fear And Confront Your Fear And Stop Avoiding It. 58

Chapter 8: Realize The Importance Of Self-Confidence 65

Chapter 9: Using Negotiations And Compromise To Resolve Conflict 71

Chapter 10: Conducting Effective Workplace Discussions 76

Chapter 11: How To Employ Diplomacy To Win Over Your Team 85

Chapter 12: Know Your Audience 91

Conclusion 98

Introduction

Contrary to popular belief, conversing may hinder your ability to effectively communicate and connect with others. On the surface, this assertion may appear absurd. But consider it in this way: You have probably experienced relationships with friends or family members in which the dynamics of the relationship changed and you were unsure of how to proceed. You had no idea what to say. If you attempted to discuss the circumstance, you were unsuccessful. It even made matters worse! Over time, nobody ever discussed the situation. It became a forbidden subject. When this occurs, sadly, silence, guilt, shame, and even judgement infiltrate the relationship. This book discusses how to stop merely talking and begin communicating more effectively with those you care about when these taboo topics arise, in order to maintain healthy, long-lasting relationships.

Full disclosure: I am a communication scientist. You may wonder what a communication scientist is and what they do. I hold a Ph.D. in communication studies with a concentration in health communication. This entails researching theories, identifying and implementing practical methods regarding how people communicate and do not communicate, what topics people are and are not willing to communicate about, what influences the ability to communicate, and how we can improve communication for understanding. I am particularly interested in what individuals will and will not discuss about their personal health, health behaviours, and disease with others and health care providers. I am curious as to why people are unwilling to discuss a disease or the emergence of new symptoms, even with medical professionals. Furthermore, if they do, what motivates them to share it and with whom? It is a science, yes. I've studied many facets of communication over the years, including interpersonal conflict, stigma in its various forms, doctor-patient communication, intercultural communication, family communication, persuasion, and disclosure, to name a few. Clearly, communication science is a vast and continuously expanding field.

In addition, I am a Black American woman born in Houston, Texas (from the Northside). Do not be fooled by education, degrees, and credentials. I am a professional, but I also know how to remove my earrings in public if necessary. I am the type of friend who would stand by you no matter what. I will take a ten-foot stance when everyone else is fleeing.

I use my voice to make the technical jargon applicable to your everyday life, using the knowledge and scientific information I've acquired. If you cannot relate to the scenarios or determine how to apply the information in this book to your life, then I have not completed my assignment. The words on these pages are not based on what I have heard or read, but on what I have experienced myself or helped others experience. Through communication, I am here to really help you become the best version of yourself.

You may be curious as to how I became aware of such a career and what motivated me to pursue a career in communication science. Well, the short answer is that I arrived here via a winding path. My path to beeasily coming a communication scientist was not direct and straightforward. Early in my life, I felt as though communication was stifled, which sparked my interest in enhancing communication. Frequently, I felt that I was not given the whole story in relationships. I was expected, and even required, to keep certain relationships' secrets. There appeared to be taboo topics, or subjects that were never to be discussed, in many of my earliest relationships. I learned at a young age what not to discuss and with whom not to converse. My speech was muffled. My opinion was irrelevant. My emotions were not taken into account. I also understood the significance of communication. Not only was it significant, but the majority of us just get it wrong. The majority of us misunderstand each other due to poor communication.

As I matured into a woman, it became abundantly clear to me that I had a voice, and that I would use it. No longer would I permit others to mute me. Today, I say and mean exactly what I mean. Period. And anyone who knows me personally will confirm that I am direct. When communicating with me, you will know exactly where you stand, and you will not be confused about my position. Consequently, honesty is one of my fundamental values. Truthful communication is also one of my core values. I pay close attention to the words I use and those others use with me.

I've always been fascinated by the necessity of communication in daily life. Communication is ubiquitous. We may even be experiencing communication overload. The list is endless: television, social media, the telephone, advertisements, movies, neighbours, the news, billboards, friends, family, and coworkers. So, if we have so many forms of communication and must communicate constantly, why do so many of us, including myself, occasionally just get it wrong? Why do we sometimes just feel unable to communicate... or that we need a "do-over" for something we said and wish we could retract?

I find it intriguing that our educational system does not include a communication curriculum. To graduate from high school, we must take English, mathematics, and numerous other required courses, but communication is rarely required. Moreover, we are not taught how communication impacts and affects our daily lives, health, and relationships, despite the fact that it does. Sure, you can take a communication course as an elective in college, and you can even choose communication as a major, but prior to college, there is no instruction or training in communication. What if you elect not to attend college?

As a result, the majority of us learn communication as we easy go along. In reality, the approach is more hit or miss. If something is successful, we continue doing it. If it doesn't, we stop. Communication is significantly more complex than that. And it is in the complexity of communication that I enjoy assisting others to take ownership. Yes, claim it.

Having said that, my communication experience extends far beyond the academic and professional levels. I also wrote this book based on my personal experience as someone who has maintained friendships with each person for at least 20 years on average. The seasons of our friendships have changed over the years. Occasionally, we have been close, and at other times, we have been distant or completely out of touch. We have found our way back to each other over time.

I also have family members with whom I am estranged and others with whom I rarely communicate. Despite the fact that you cannot choose your relatives, there is good value in connecting and forming relationships with those who share your ancestry. Some of the most pressing questions about who we are, why we do what we do, why we think the way we think, and the source of our talents and natural abilities can be answered by reflecting on family relationships. Yes, family relationships are crucial, but they can also be among the most difficult to maintain. I acknowledge that I have not always been correct. But I've discovered strategies you can use in your relationships with friends and family to turn the tide on these challenging topics.

Chapter 1: Easy Ways To Improve Relationship Communication

During our first three weeks together, we engaged in sontantlu. We were so focused on the bickering (rather than what we were actually arguing about) that we ended up arguing about how we were bickering! Have a headache immediately? Yes, we had one for approximately three weeks. We finally sat down and had a discussion because we are not that bitter.

We had to learn a new way of interacting with each other because we were sharing the same language. We discussed the things that ultimately mattered (such as how to spend our money) and the things that ultimately did not matter (such as who takes out the trash). We would have never known what actually mattered to the other person if we hadn't sat down and talked about it.

In the end, we realised that none of our complaints were about the issues we were fighting for, but rather about not feeling heard or respected. From that day forward, we decided to have a weekly "aeon" where we set aside an hour to freely express our thoughts. This enables you to just feel heard and revitalised.

Obviously, our hour-long lunch break may not work for everyone, but it does for us. Because of our Bae Sessions, we've been able to avoid larger crowds, actively listen to one another, form bonds, and just feel closer to one another. We may speak every day, but we're both so busy with work and life that it makes sense to set aside time for something a little more involved.

6. Tell Them What You Really want From Them Sometimes I just really want to vent and just feel validated when my partner laughs and says, "Yeah, that really does make me just feel bad!" Other times, I desire advice. Like I've

mentioned before that none of you are mind readers, so it's important to keep your partner informed so you're all on the same page. Saying something in advance such as "I need to vent right now and I'm not looking for any advice, just your support" or "I really need your advice on this situation" will let them know precisely what you require at that time.

Being clear about what you require can also alleviate some of the communication or stress in a given situation. By informing them in advance, we may be able to prevent those unnecessary disagreements caused by a communication.

Communication is an Ability

Immunization is a skill, which means there is always room for improvement. Determine with your partner how you can maintain healthy communication and remain on the same page. Be as sincere, respectful, kind, and considerate as you can. Whether it's a bae session or mrlu making a greater effort to warm up to each other.

Chapter 2: Methods To A Resolution

Entering into a conflict situation is the simplest aspect of life, as it is frequently unintentional. Extricating yourself from a tense situation, however, requires a great deal more finesse and grace, as well as an array of skills to ensure that the situation does not escalate.

Reacting to Criticism Made of You

Even if there are no flaws, someone will always find something to criticise, regardless of how hard you try to please everyone all the time. Depending on the volatility of your temper, you will either disregard it as a minor annoyance or respond in kind.

Criticism Described

We are acquainted with two varieties of criticism. The first is constructive, while the second is negative.

Positive and negative feedback are permitted by constructive criticism, but both are designed and delivered in a way that promotes growth and enhanced performance. This can be provided by a loved one or a supervisor regarding a particular project.

Negative criticism inhibits growth and is frequently perceived as insulting and demeaning, undermining the time and effort invested in a project.

Criticism is an essential component of the work performed, particularly when a team has become unproductive or complacent. It is inevitable that you will receive criticism, some of which will be fair and some not, and there are ways to deal with it.

Controlling your reaction—your work ethic will be determined by your response to criticism, and specifically by your level of professionalism; this includes your body language more than your words. To avoid a reflexive response, take a deep breath and count to five while maintaining facial control.

Don't take it personally; because we devote so much of ourselves to our work, we frequently take criticism personally. When you are able to separate yourself from your work, you will realise that your professional mistakes do not define you as a person.

If you internalise criticism and fail to analyse what it means objectively, you will become defensive and make excuses instead of using the feedback to improve yourself. When you implement these changes, you demonstrate your maturity and capacity for self-reflection.

Recognize your humanity; making mistakes is part of being human, and everyone, whether novice or expert, will fail. It is essential to acknowledge that it occurred and, as stated previously, to find a way to take corrective action.

Be appreciative; it's not always simple to sincerely thank someone for their feedback, especially if it's sincere and intended to really help you rather than to tear you down. It was likely just as awkward for them as it was for you.

Be humble; when you pause before responding to criticism, you are able to analyse the feedback and acknowledge the possibility that their words contain some truth. Even if your eeasy go has been wounded, you can only benefit from the experience.

Give a simple apology; simply apologise with no explanations unless the conversation calls for them. A profuse apology could appear insincere and make the conversation uncomfortable.

You have a tendency to dwell on things you perceive as negative, and you tend to internalise the negative instead of focusing on the positive; this prevents you from altering your behaviour to improve your performance.

Changing Your Attitude Toward Criticism

When receiving feedback, focus on what is true and disregard what does not apply to you personally, especially if the feedback pertains to a team project. Utilize the negative aspects of the feedback in order to improve your performance. There are multiple ways to find the positive in any given feedback:

Who is the critic? In the vast majority of cases, your colleagues really want the best results for your work and really want to really help you improve. This will really help you identify areas for improvement.

Self-awareness is essential—acknowledge that the criticism hurt and investigate the reasons why so that you can heal, especially if it is related to your past.

Listen to what is being said; rather than hearing the words to defend yourself, listen so that you can interpret the meaning of the words and use them to your advantage.

Respect the criticism; negative criticism can be just as valuable as positive criticism and can have a greater impact on your work ethic because it affects a change opportunity.

Use the feedback as a learning opportunity and, as difficult as it may be, try not to let it affect your confidence. Utilize this opportunity to observe how criticism affects you and how it can assist you in the future when you must provide feedback.

Commentary on the Workplace

Your team requires feedback to ensure they are on the right path. This allows the team to make the necessary modifications to a project to ensure everyone's satisfaction. When they do not receive any feedback, whether constructive or not, they will either assume the project is perfect and continue as they were, or they will determine that it is not worth their time or effort to provide feedback.

When Is Criticism Excessive?

When the criticism is insulting or demeaning and there is nothing constructive in their feedback, it is neither constructive nor even mildly negative. It may border on a possible personal attack and can stem from a variety of sources, such as the other person's jealousy, insecurity, or guilt. You must remember that you have no control over it, and that even though it is directed at you, it is not about you. When the communication is humiliating or could harm your reputation, it is best to find an objective third party to really help you have a conversation with the offender, as this could be considered bullying. You could be targeted for a variety of reasons:

A supervisor or manager may exert pressure regarding your performance.

You are the person who calls attention to improper conduct.

Your work ethic or standard is superior to that of your teammate.

The person will intentionally threaten you with harm.

Chapter 3: The Art Of Communicating Your Thoughts And Emotions Across Various Mediums.

Have you ever been told to do something but had no idea how to do it and found it extremely difficult to convey this? The person you are speaking with is also making things difficult for themselves. Perhaps they just feel similarly that they are not being heard, or they may be in a position where they do not wish to have their feelings hurt.

Our jobs require us to be able to articulate ideas clearly and concisely, so it is not surprising that communication skills are so important. Yet it is astounding how many of us do not know how to do this properly. It is essential to comprehend another person's tone of voice and body language in order to effectively convey your message. In a conversation, our tone, word choice, and body language can indicate whether we are friendly or hostile towards the other person.

Communicating your thoughts and feelings across different mediums, particularly during a conversation, is crucial, but there are two components that must be executed correctly:

First, you must assess the mental and emotional state of the person you are speaking with to ensure they are in an optimal state for conversation. This is accomplished by observing their body language and vocal tone. This will convey that you are concerned for the other person's wellbeing.

Your tone of voice is essential for consistent communication with what you are saying. If you speak in a monotone or appear uninterested, the other person will become bored or will not take you seriously.

Second, as you begin to discuss this issue or topic, consider what the other person needs to hear and how you can demonstrate it. The best method for doing so is through storytelling. When we tell stories, we use words that stir our emotions and evoke images in the minds of others. Most of us don't like to hear that we're boring or that our stories are boring, so it's crucial to paint a vivid picture and provide relevant examples to make your story engaging.

Many individuals fear public speaking because they believe they are inadequate or will say the wrong thing. As soon as you master your communication skills, you won't have to worry about this anymore! If speaking in front of a group makes you uncomfortable, try practising in front of a mirror or with friends and family. When you are comfortable and just feel more confident, you can begin practising on others. Remember, if you really want people to listen to your opinion/proposal, it must be concise and compelling. Avoid equivocation and just get straight to the point.

If you just feel that you are not being listened to during a conversation, stop speaking, look away from the other person, and consider how you can be more direct. This will really help them understand your message better.

This will only be successful if done with respect. If you have rolled your eyes or laughed at what they have said, they will interpret this as a sign that you don't care or that they should take a break so their feelings won't be hurt. Remember that you are initiating the conversation, and it is not your responsibility to constantly correct others. If you are attempting to persuade someone of something, you are responsible for getting them to agree with you.

Another way to enhance your communication skills is to determine whether the other person is beeasily coming bored. If so, repeat what they've said in different words or express your opinion on the matter. People will be more inclined to converse with you in the future if they see that you are genuinely interested in them.

Acronym-laden topics will be difficult for those unfamiliar with the subject. It is prudent to utilise your past experiences in your current endeavours. If you are attempting to convey something but using a large number of adjectives, the message will be lost because the words are unrelated.

When communicating with others, you must be honest and genuine; people have a sixth sense for detecting when someone is being dishonest, which makes them hesitant to interact with that person again. This can cause issues in your relationship if they misinterpret it (they'll assume you don't like them or they didn't speak as much).

A second perspective on communication skills is that everyone makes mistakes and we always learn from them. It is essential to learn from your mistakes and develop new, effective methods of communication with others.

If you are having trouble communicating with someone, avoid harsh judgement. If someone uses inappropriate language or acts aggressively toward you, you should not judge them or put yourself in their shoes. Depression and low self-esteem are just two of the many mental health issues that can make it difficult for a person to communicate effectively if they have had a difficult childhood.

Possibly the other person is under a great deal of stress and feels that you do not understand them; this could be a result of their communication style. If you don't know how to communicate with someone in your life, you should educate yourself on what they're going through. This will really help you learn how to communicate effectively with that individual, so they will just feel more comfortable sharing their thoughts and emotions.

To effectively communicate, we must first listen. By listening, we can give the other person our undivided attention and refrain from allowing our thoughts to cloud our judgement or disrupt what they are saying. They must just feel that when they speak with you, you are attentive to what they have to say. To accomplish this, repeat and summarise what the other person has said and determine whether or not this makes sense.

In order for the other person to know that we're interested in them, it's also important to compliment or express our feelings during the conversation. If they are not listened to and believe that no one else cares about them, they will not discuss their emotions with others again.

You can also look at another person's face while they are speaking to demonstrate your body language and interest in what they are saying. The more you practise these techniques, the more effective your conversations will become, and the more effectively you will be able to communicate with others.

Communication issues are a common source of arguments and conflict, but they also present us with an opportunity to learn how to communicate more effectively. When people disagree with our ideas, new points of view, or what we have to say, it is crucial not to display anger, irritation, or annoyance. Remember that most people will not become angry if you explain your position clearly and demonstrate why it is in their best interest.

By repeating, paraphrasing, and summarising a person's point of view, we can demonstrate that we are interested in what they are saying. By observing their face and body language while they speak, we will have a better understanding of how they feel. Instead of ignoring their frowns or gestures, we should check with them to see if something is wrong or inquire as to why they are unhappy.

When someone says something that is difficult for us to hear or comprehend, we should avoid reacting as if it were a surprise; otherwise, they may misinterpret our reaction.

Even if we disagree, we should be courteous when questioning a person's viewpoint. This demonstrates their commitment to their position, allowing us to take them seriously.

If someone is pushing to make an argument, we should not engage in a physical altercation but instead use our words to state the facts and explain why we disagree with them. When people express their opinion too quickly, they may not have given it sufficient consideration. Before attempting to persuade them otherwise, we must determine why they just feel so strongly about the issue.

If someone is overly aggressive towards us when we disagree with their ideas, we should attempt to reason with them. By demonstrating your unwillingness to engage in physical conflict, you can convey your message without resorting to violence. If they just feel insulted, it is understandable that they will just feel annoyed or hostile, but this does not mean that you must argue back or disregard their emotions.

The purpose of communication is not only to effectively express our ideas and persuade the other person; it is also to work as a team. We may not agree on all topics, but we can agree that what we have to say is for the greater good.

Transparency, honesty, and sincerity are fundamental aspects of communication. If you initially lack confidence, do not panic. It is preferable to begin communicating effectively, even if this is not your strong suit, than to remain silent and leave someone confused as to why you are unresponsive.

Before communicating with another person, prepare to demonstrate your interest in them and their ideas. To be a more effective communicator, you must actively consider what others are saying while listening. Pay attention to the speaker's intonation, tone, and facial expression in order to comprehend what they are saying.

If you listen attentively, you will make it easier for the other person to express their feelings and communicate with us. To understand the other person's feelings, we should put ourselves in their shoes when communicating with them.

When we listen attentively, it is easier to express our ideas or add something of good value that no one else has said, because we understand what they are experiencing.

What valid reasons do you have for avoiding communication?

Sometimes we may just feel hesitant to interact with others, but this is not necessarily a negative trait. We should only communicate with those who really want to hear what we have to say; if we do not see this as necessary, it is irrelevant if others do.

For example, we may believe that those around us are not listening attentively enough. They may appear uninterested in what we have to say or interrupt our conversations when we speak. If this is the case, we should avoid them because they will distract us from what we're attempting to concentrate on.

There are additional reasons why we shouldn't communicate with someone, such as a lack of shared interests or incompatibility with our desired way of life. If we just feel uncomfortable when speaking with someone because they are too aggressive, it may not be worthwhile to speak with them every time they really want to speak with us.

Regardless of the reason for avoiding communication with someone, it is generally preferable to avoid them.

By observing how others communicate, you can learn how to communicate more effectively yourself. If you really want to positively influence someone, you must understand how to become more effective at doing so.

By observing a person's behaviour, you will be able to discern their apparent interests and passions. You may also be able to tell when someone is going through a difficult time in their life, but you can demonstrate your concern by asking how they're doing or offering assistance.

We may learn from others so long as we refrain from copying or imitating them, as this could just get us into trouble. We should pay attention to the words and body language of others in order to effectively communicate with others.

There are numerous resources available to really help us communicate effectively with others. By reading stories, studies, and books about famous authors and public speakers, we can also gain insight into how to effectively communicate. By analysing their behaviour and the way they express themselves, we can increase our vocabulary and become more expressive.

When we're ready to speak with another person, our body language must be open so that the other person is not distracted from what we're saying. If we just feel nervous, we should stand tall and smile so as not to make others just feel uneasy.

We may lack confidence in how we discuss our ideas and influences, but that does not preclude us from making improvements. It is easy to become distracted by other people or our own thoughts, but if someone attempts to explain something to us clearly, we should be receptive.

If you're self-conscious about your speech, you should engage in conversation with others. By conversing with others, we can learn how they express their ideas and react to our responses; therefore, we must spend time conversing with others so they can provide us with feedback on the effectiveness of our communication.

When engaging in conversation with another person, we should strive to listen as attentively as they do. Especially if this is the case, this can be challenging because we may just feel they are not interested in what we have to say or are talking over us. By observing others, we can improve our interpersonal relationships.

If our communication skills are unclear, there is no point in attempting to discuss an issue, as this could leave people confused. We should encourage these individuals so that they will assist us in enhancing our ability to communicate our ideas and influences.

We cannot change something in which we lack confidence, but we can be receptive to the feedback of others in order to gain confidence. The best way to do this is to ask people what they think of our ideas, but sometimes we should also listen and ask for advice or suggestions on how to express ourselves.

Chapter 4: The Influence Of Self-Esteem

Confidence is a crucial component of effective public speaking. Confidence can really help individuals engage an audience, effectively communicate their message, and handle challenging questions and situations.

Here are several ways in which confidence can influence public speaking:

Engaging the audience: Confidence can assist individuals in establishing a rapport with the audience and maintaining their interest.

Confidence can assist individuals in delivering their message in a clear and persuasive manner.

Handling difficult questions and situations: Confidence can assist individuals in navigating difficult questions and situations with poise and composure.

Confidence can really help individuals manage and overcome stage fright, enabling them to deliver a successful public speaking performance.

There are numerous ways to improve public speaking confidence. Some strategies include thorough preparation, rehearsal, the use of relaxation techniques, and seeking assistance from friends, family, or a public speaking coach.

Overall, self-assurance is a crucial component of effective public speaking. Individuals can effectively engage an audience and deliver successful public speaking performances by gaining confidence through preparation and practise.

Experience and self-acceptance are significant factors in easily developing public speaking confidence.

As individuals gain experience with public speaking, they are able to develop their skills and techniques and just grow more confident in their abilities. Regular practise and delivery of speeches can really help individuals develop confidence over time.

Accepting oneself and one's limitations can also aid in the development of public speaking confidence. Instead of focusing on perfection or attempting to be someone else, it is essential to embrace one's unique qualities and strengths. By accepting and embracing oneself, individuals can develop self-assurance and deliver more authentic and engaging public speeches.

Here are some strategies for gaining self-assurance through experience and acceptance of oneself:

Practice frequently: The more a person practises public speaking, the more comfortable and assured they will become.

Seek feedback: Receiving feedback from others, such as friends, family, or a public speaking coach, can assist individuals in identifying areas for improvement and boosting their self-confidence.

Instead of attempting to be someone else, it is essential to embrace one's unique qualities and strengths. This can assist individuals in delivering more authentic and engaging public speeches.

Accept imperfections: It is normal to make errors and have flaws. Instead of dwelling on them, it is essential to accept them and move on. This can aid individuals in gaining confidence and delivering more natural and genuine public speeches.

Confidence is a crucial success factor when it comes to public speaking. Confidence can aid individuals in effectively communicating their message, engaging their audience, and handling difficult questions and situations. Consequently, individuals who have confidence in their public speaking skills are more likely to have successful presentations.

Here are some ways in which confidence can contribute to public speaking success:

Confidence can assist individuals in engaging the audience: Confidence can assist individuals in establishing a rapport with the audience and maintaining their attention. This can enhance the effectiveness and appeal of the presentation.

Confidence can aid individuals in effectively communicating their message. Confidence can aid individuals in delivering their message clearly and persuasively. This can increase the audience's likelihood of comprehending and remembering the message.

Confidence can aid individuals in handling difficult questions and situations: Confidence can aid individuals in navigating difficult questions and situations with poise and composure. This can assist people in preserving their credibility and reputation.

Confidence can aid in overeasily coming stage fright: Confidence can really help individuals manage and overcome stage fright, enabling them to give a successful public speech.

Overall, self-assurance is a crucial success factor when it comes to public speaking. Individuals can deliver successful public speaking performances and achieve their goals if they develop their confidence through preparation and practise.

Chapter 5: Learn How To Good Value Your Children In Public.

In any case, would it be prudent for you to generally avoid praise? No, you only need to meticulously direct it. Careful recognition can be an extraordinary addition to your collection of nurturing tools. Therefore, the next time you wish to laud your child, try substituting the following expressions for your usual ones.

Here are 10 examples of effective recognition proclamations to try with your child:

Rather than saying "Well done!"

Attempt: "I appreciate your assistance with the cleanup. I particularly admire the manner in which the shoes have been arranged. This will have a significant impact on our efforts to locate our shoes at the beginning of the day.

One of the keys to more powerful applause is being explicit. "Great job" is imprecise because it does not specify what the child did to earn your praise, it does not provide constructive criticism, and it does not indicate what behaviour they should adopt in the future.

Related: why you should really praise yourself in front of your children, mother

Specify precisely what you are happy about. Mention why it satisfied you, with the hope that they will repeat it in the future. Specifically, explicitness helps them to just feel respected.

Rather than saying "You did it!"

"I have observed you attempting to tie your shoelaces for quite some time. It's precarious, right? Nevertheless, I am pleased that you persisted and did not give up. I'm confident that you'll just get it soon with your training and perseverance!"

Acknowledge the effort, not the outcome. Rapidly demoralise and demotivate a child by focusing solely on accomplishments. It is acceptable to commend achievement, but it is more important to commend the work that preceded that achievement. Applauding effort convinces and demonstrates confidence in the child.

Rather than saying "You look so beautiful!"

Try: "I adore the creatures on your T-shirt; which is your favourite? Why is that the case?

Adulating children, especially young women, for their appearance can diminish their confidence. They may begin to believe that people like them solely because of their appearance, which can lead to a tremendous amount of tension as they age.

Appropriating a child's appearance can unintentionally associate their identity with their appearance. To compliment a child's appearance, emphasise what the child can change. For instance, use the child's clothing to spark a conversation that demonstrates your genuine interest in what they think and feel.

Rather than saying "That is an exceptional drawing!"

Attempt: "Wow, I adore the variety you've chosen for the flowers; why did you decide to paint them in that colour?"

This year, you may have viewed a hundred works of art, but to your child, each is extraordinary and new. Despite the fact that it may be simpler to state, "This is an excellent drawing" without actually examining it, what matters most to children is that they examine the artwork properly.

Choosing portions of the image and requesting information about their decisions demonstrates that you are genuinely interested in and appreciative of their work. Which, in kid parlance, translates to you noticing and valuing them.

5. Rather than "Going method, buddy!"

Attempt: "You really exerted so much effort on that piece of work. I am pleased that your instructor has recognised this. You deserve that grade. Is there anything you've learned from this article that you can later apply to your own work?"

Observe your child's behaviour if he or she focuses. Let them know you observed their sincere effort and that their work was valued. When they receive a passing grade, instead of simply praising the result, discuss with them what went well. This is an exceptional opportunity to really help future school by requiring the student to consider the cycles and activities that led to the passing grade and to apply them again in the future.

Instead of "Outstanding young lady!"

"You worked diligently on that numerical question. I realise you could address it if you were genuinely interested!"

Commending children for fixed credits, such as intelligence or aptitude in specific subjects, can backfire. Not only will children avoid making a solid effort in the future if they believe they are naturally good at something, but they will also become immediately frustrated if they encounter difficulty, assuming they are intelligent all things considered.

Instead of "That was courteous of you!"

Attempt: "When that young man fell, I saw you assist him. He must have been extremely irritated, right? However, I believe that by giving him a hug, you helped him to just feel significantly better. It feels better to really help individuals, doesn't it?"

Again, this relates to observing what your child has done and communicating to them that you have observed and appreciated their activities by depicting what you have observed. Requesting that the child consider how they just feel about their positive actions as a whole increases the likelihood that they will be repeated in the future.

Instead of: "Yahoo, you pooped in the toilet!"

Try this: "You defecated in the toilet! I'm aware that you tried a few times today but were unsuccessful, but all of your practise has helped, hasn't it? Now you've discovered how to make it happen!"

Potty training and applause will often remain closely linked, but praising children for their 'accomplishments' can backfire in this case. First, they may exert themselves to complete a task when they do not have to. Here, the recognition can assist them in ignoring their body's symptoms and eliminating them in order to be commended. This is not exactly what is required for potty preparation.

Related: Ten positive nurturing techniques for child restraint

Second, applauding results overlooks all the effort put in, regardless of whether they were unable to complete a task or make it to the bathroom on time. However, it is this effort that brought them to their destination. Indeed, regardless of errors, focus on the work itself and not the outcome.

Instead of "Yahoo, you've finally finished your dinner!"

Try: "I assume you're not eager right now; that's fine. I'll put this food in the microwave; let me know if you really want me to warm it up for you later.

Perhaps the most counterproductive praise is commending for eating. It encourages adolescents to stop listening to everything their bodies are saying. They discover that it is beneficial to eat when they are not eager to please others and to consume foods they could do without in order to just feel significantly better. Over time, these eating behaviours can quickly lead to bingeing, comfort eating, and eating at home. Keep praise far away from the dinner table.

Instead of "Great job on quieting down!"

Attempt: "Were you actually frantic? It is acceptable to be angry at times. You will develop more techniques for maintaining composure as you age. Up until then, I'm eager to really help you quiet down."

Complimenting children when they are "great" and ignoring them when they are "terrible" can lead to a variety of problems. When children are frantic, they do not lose their temper for no apparent reason. They're angry because they're not feeling better, and they have no control over their emotions. Loading up on praise when they are quiet is like telling them, "I really like you."

Chapter 6: How To Enhance Your Conversational Iq

Do not dominate: a discussion in which one person dominates and prevents others from speaking is not a discussion at all. It implies that you do not respect the other person's opinions and, therefore, them.

In addition, such dominance may cause irritability and agitation, which triggers the release of the stress hormone cortisol. As a result, they become less receptive to what you say and less likely to participate in the project or provide future suggestions.

- Connect through listening: In conversations, people often fail to truly listen to one another because they are waiting for the perfect moment to speak, assert their authority, or formulate a response. They are able to evaluate the other person's ideas in light of their own. But when you listen attentively and make an effort to comprehend the other person, you foster trust and enhance communication, thereby strengthening bonds.

Many of us are "addicted to being right," and it may just feel good to believe we have all the answers in a discussion about a business project. - Keep an open mind. This can aid us in advancing our position and expediting resolutions. By focusing solely on our own perspective, however, we miss the opportunity to explore other perspectives and maximise the potential for team cooperation and co-creation. Therefore, be curious and seek information when you don't know the answer; learn how others view potential solutions and alternative approaches to a problem. It will encourage conversation and the exchange of ideas, which will ultimately benefit everyone.

A higher level of conversational intelligence may result in improved communication and relationships, which can be advantageous to you and your organisation. Conversation is an essential leadership competency.

Chapter 7: How To Manage Anxiety And Fear And Confront Your Fear And Stop Avoiding It.

If fear has the upper hand, you may stop doing the things you need to do or the activities that make you happy. You avoid it out of fear of discovering the truth for yourself. Due to the fear, anxiety develops over time, which is undesirable. To be able to handle this situation, you must take a stand and confront your concerns. You can learn to regulate it by exposing yourself to it occasionally. Try to confront whatever is bothering you, be it a fear of snakes, a breakup, your parents, or weight loss.

Knowledge of Oneself

Determine the root cause of your fear and anxiety. Keep a journal in which you can record your thoughts during stressful situations. Invest some time in discovering the causes of the journal entries you've made. Instead of avoiding these things, you should make an effort to face them. Also record the activities you use to reduce your anxiety. As your understanding of what causes your anxiety and fear increases, so do your chances of gaining control over them.

Exercising

Home or gym-based exercise can be beneficial. It helps eliminate fear and anxiety by enhancing mental concentration and fortitude. The brain releases hormones that reduce fear and anxiety during exercise.

Relaxing

Using a relaxation technique to reduce anxiety and fear can be extremely beneficial. During a period of relaxation, the mind becomes tranquil and mental strength increases. It consists of raising and lowering the shoulder while inhaling and exhaling deeply. Visualize yourself on vacation, perhaps lying on a beach on an island, as a means of relaxation. Yoga and meditation, when practised, can also yield beneficial results.

Consumption of nutritious foods This can be achieved by eating an abundance of fruits and vegetables rather than fast food. Reduce your consumption of sugary beverages and coffee. It is common knowledge that drinking coffee may increase anxiety.

Reduce your consumption of alcohol.

Some individuals believe that alcohol will assist them in overeasily coming or coping with their problems. Widespread is the practise of drinking when anxious. Abuse of alcohol will not only exacerbate anxiety problems, but will also increase fear and anxiety. Alcohol does not give you courage; programming your emotions to do so does.

Spirituality and God Belief

Using the spiritual technique, others can connect with something they just feel was missing. You can cope by adhering to the teachings of your religion during stressful situations and when facing challenges.

Participating in counselling sessions

By participating in therapy sessions, one may decide to obtain professional assistance. If your fear and anxiety are out of control and you are unable to manage them on your own, therapy can help. CBT, also known as cognitive behavioural therapy, is a treatment option that can be utilised. Throughout the sessions, numerous activities are performed to aid the individual in coping.

Medication Although it is known that medications only reduce fear and anxiety, they can also be used to manage these feelings. This solution is not permanent. It provides only a temporary solution and does not address the underlying causes of fear and anxiety. A person may choose to use drugs while searching for alternative coping mechanisms.

Assist Teams

There are others who experience fear and anxiety in the same way as you do. It can be quite advantageous to attend a gathering with these individuals. Some of these individuals have already mastered the art of fear management, so conversing with them about fear can really help you learn more about its management. The committee has gathered these individuals so they can face their challenges together. The meeting includes personal accounts, advice on overeasily coming anxiety and fear, and motivational words from those who have accomplished this feat. As opposed to those who are unfamiliar with your situation, hearing stories from people who are similar to you creates a wonderful feeling and a bond.

Adopt An Upbeat Attitude

Discover how to cultivate a positive outlook. A negative mindset promotes anxiety and fear, so think only of positive things. Engage in activities that bring you joy and increase the pleasure in your life. Watching comedies with your family, engaging in enjoyable activities with your friends, and going to the beach with your family are all enjoyable activities.

Chapter 8: Realize The Importance Of Self-Confidence

Successful negotiators share a common trait of self-assurance. They always appear in charge of themselves and their negotiation contacts. How can you attain this air of confidence? Before meeting with your adversaries, carefully consider your alternatives to settlement. Once you comprehend your options, you will no longer just feel fear. Your self-assurance is likely to influence your fellow negotiators. If your competitors believe that their non-settlement options are less appealing than the options available to you, they will be under greater pressure to negotiate. This is when they begin to make greater and greater concessions.

When your self-confidence begins to wane, which happens to even the most self-confident among us, and you begin to doubt your negotiating skills, you should do two things:

Consider the weaknesses of your opponents so that you can exploit what they are concealing. They are highlighting their strengths, and you must guess what flaws they are concealing.

2. reevaluate your own situation to determine which of your strengths you are showcasing. If you do a good job of concealing your own weaknesses, your competitors may assume you have greater strength than you actually do. Reconsider your non-settlement options and concentrate on the alternatives available to your opponents. Avoid giving your opponent false strength.

When I serve as a negotiator's consultant for attorneys, they do a fantastic job of highlighting their own side's flaws. When I put myself in their opponents' shoes and explain the challenges they face, the attorneys with whom I work are stunned. They have completely ignored the obstacles that their opponents face. At this time, they begin to recognise their negotiating strength.

When making concessions, adhere to your principles. Position adjustments must be strategically planned and communicated. When used appropriately, a concession can convey both a cooperative attitude and sufficient firmness to suggest the need for a counteroffer if the negotiator wishes to continue the negotiation process. Intelligent negotiators begin the distributive phase with principled positions that logically justify their desires. Make principled concessions that you can adequately defend to your competitors. When placing a new position on the table, provide an explanation for your decision. You can argue that you undervalued or overvalued a particular item by a certain amount, and then adjust your current position accordingly. You may also say that you failed to thoroughly analyse a crucial piece of information and then change your current offer appropriately.

This strategy causes you to stop at your counterpart's new position rather than a higher or lower one, and it causes them to wonder if their own positions are still legitimate or need to be revised.

When a surrender is made unexpectedly, it indicates nervousness and a lack of control. This is particularly true when a position shift is made tentatively and unprincipledly by someone who continues to speak uncomfortably and defensively after the compromise. Such action indicates a lack of confidence and informs the other party that the individual who has just switched positions does not anticipate rapid reciprocity. When you come across such concession-makers, gently urge them to keep talking, since this method frequently results in more unanswered concessions. You should be able to capture control of the interaction and generate good outcomes if you can encourage rivals to bid against themselves via successive position alterations. \sAs soon as the concession is revealed, you should remain silent and wait for a suitable reaction from your opponent. If none is fortheasily coming right away, calmly wait for the receiving person to resume the conversation. This informs him or her that you will not take any additional action until your first movement is reciprocated.

Time your concessions carefully

Concessions must be made at the right time. When you move too rapidly, you seem too eager, and opponents will interpret this as a sign of weakness. You convey weakness if you make continuous compromises—or unduly generous ones. You must be patient and avoid moving too rapidly. To prevent bidding against yourself, make sure your opponent reciprocates your position modifications. Persons who are unwilling to make compromises when position changes are anticipated, on the other hand, are likely to irritate their colleagues and lead them to believe that further discussions would be futile. As a result, such inactivity may destabilise the whole negotiation process.

Chapter 9: Using Negotiations And Compromise To Resolve Conflict

As disagreements arise naturally when parenting, good parenting requires the ability to compromise and negotiate. When disputes erupt, parents must approach the matter calmly, with an open mind, and with a willingness to hear what their kid has to say. Parents may assist their children to learn critical problem-solving skills and really help to develop a deeper and more loving connection by negotiating and compromising with them.

The process of establishing rules and limits with a kid may serve as an illustration of how to use negotiation and compromise to settle a problem.

Children naturally desire to challenge norms and limitations as they attempt to establish their independence. Parents may utilize negotiation to just get a mutually agreeable set of rules that both the parent and the kid are comfortable with rather than merely imposing rules without the youngster's involvement. The youngster may communicate their wants and needs throughout this process, and the parent may share their worries and justifications. Both sides may reach a solution that considers the needs and viewpoints of the parent and the kid via this approach.

When establishing limits and rules with a kid, for example, compromise and bargaining may be useful. For instance, a parent could set a time for their kid to just get home from school on weeknights so that they can just get adequate rest for class.

The youngster could, nonetheless, choose to remain out later to spend time with buddies. In this circumstance, the parent maybe attempt to compromise with the youngster by outlining their worries for their welfare and the good value of a good night's sleep.

Additionally, they could propose a compromise, such as letting the kid stay out longer on the weekends or special occasions. The parent and kid may prevent a conflict and keep their connection strong and happy by talking things out and easily coming up with a solution that works for both of them.

Making decisions on family tasks or chores may serve as another illustration of how to employ negotiation and compromise to settle a problem. If they are assigned too many tasks or if they believe the obligations are unjust, children may just feel overburdened or resentful.

Parents may assist to avoid disputes and foster a greater feeling of collaboration and teamwork within the family by negotiating with the kid and finding methods to distribute tasks in a manner that is fair and doable for both sides.

When choosing family activities or trips, discussions, and compromise maybe be helpful in another situation. For instance, a parent could wish to easy go on a nature trek with the family, while the youngster maybe really want to visit a theme park instead. In this situation, the parent maybe bargain with the youngster by outlining the advantages of spending time in nature and stressing the need for exercise. Alternatively, they may find a middle ground by recommending that the family participate in both activities on separate days or by figuring out how to combine aspects of both hobbies into a single excursion.

The parent and kid may benefit from shared experiences and strengthen their relationship by just taking into account each other's preferences and easily coming up with a solution that suits everyone.

In addition to employing negotiation and compromise to settle individual disputes, parents should set a good example for their children by adopting these strategies. Parents may assist their kids in easily developing the skills necessary to successfully manage disputes as they just grow and mature by modeling how to discuss and resolve problems calmly and courteously.

Building a solid and loving connection with your kid requires the ability to negotiate and compromise when there are disagreements. You may assist your kid in easily developing the problem-solving abilities necessary to successfully manage disputes throughout their life by attentively listening to your child's point of view, being open to compromise, and modeling these skills for your child.

Chapter 10: Conducting Effective Workplace Discussions

One of the most important skills a leader, manager, or even a regular employee must possess is the ability to have productive conversations in the workplace. This competency is crucial for effective communication, collaboration, and problem-solving within an organisation. To be successful, these discussions must be conducted in an open and respectful manner, with ample opportunity for all participants to express their thoughts and opinions.

Ensure that all participants are included and treated with respect as the primary factor in facilitating successful workplace conversations. Regardless of experience level or position within the organisation, everyone's contribution should be valued and encouraged. In addition, it is essential to establish ground rules at the beginning of the discussion so that everyone knows what is expected of them. The ground rules may include refraining from interrupting others, staying on topic, and allowing each participant equal time to speak without interruptions.

Setting a clear agenda that outlines the conversation's objectives and the timeframes for achieving each objective is an additional important aspect of conducting successful workplace conversations. This will ensure that all participants remain focused on the desired outcomes of the discussion and provide a structure that keeps everyone on track throughout the process.

In addition, it is essential for leaders or managers leading such discussions to maintain an open mind throughout the entire process, regardless of any preconceived notions they may have about how things should proceed or what solutions may be most appropriate for the issue at hand. Encouraging brainstorming sessions where new ideas can emerge ensures that both sides come away with something constructive from their conversation, even if no consensus is initially reached, which makes it easier to come up with effective solutions in the future when additional progress must be made on specific topics discussed in initial meetings.

Lastly, it is crucial that leaders or managers take notes during these conversations so they can review details discussed before making decisions related to topics discussed during these meetings – this will also help those involved remember specifics better in the future when reviewing past discussions to determine possible next steps or strategies related to the same topics / issues discussed previously.

Effective workplace conversations are crucial for effective communication, collaboration, and problem-solving in an organisation. To ensure that these discussions remain effective and fruitful, it is essential to establish ground rules up front, establish a clear agenda in advance, and encourage brainstorming sessions. In addition, taking notes during these meetings is essential for future reference and decision-making, as well as for helping those involved remember specifics better in the future when reviewing past discussions to determine possible next steps or strategies pertaining to the same topics / issues discussed during these meetings.

A. Small Talk in the Workplace

Small talk at the office can be an important way to build relationships and foster a pleasant, friendly environment. Small talk is an often-neglected component of effective communication, but it can be used to break the ice and make people feel more comfortable in the workplace. Here are some tips for making office small talk:

Prepare topics in advance: Consider some conversational topics you could bring up in advance. Current events, news stories, sports teams, hobbies, and travel experiences all serve as excellent conversation starters. Consider browsing websites such as Reddit and Buzzfeed for conversation-starting topics to share with your coworkers.

Ask open-ended questions. Asking open-ended questions keeps conversations flowing naturally and allows your coworkers to freely express themselves without feeling interrogated or bombarded with information. Try asking questions that begin with "What" or "How" as opposed to those that require a simple yes or no response, such as "Are you enjoying your job?"

3. Listen attentively: When someone is speaking, pay close attention and maintain eye contact while nodding in agreement. If there are topics to which you can relate or that you have personal experience, don't be afraid to join the conversation! The key is not only hearing what others have to say, but also comprehending it so that you can formulate appropriate responses (and remember details from previous conversations).

It goes without saying that courtesy should always take precedence when engaging in small talk at work. Be mindful of how your words may affect others by avoiding controversial topics such as politics and religion unless specifically requested by a coworker who is clearly comfortable discussing them; otherwise, steer clear! Lastly, try not to dominate conversations; respect other people's time by being aware of their need for space, if required!

Small talk in the workplace can be an effective means of fostering relationships and fostering a positive work environment. With a little bit of practise, you'll soon feel completely at ease engaging in casual conversations with your coworkers and establishing connections that will significantly contribute to bringing the workplace closer together.

B. Effectively Communicating with Colleagues and Supervisors

Effective communication is a necessity in any workplace. To ensure that your relationships with your coworkers and manager are successful, here are some communication tips:

Ensure that you are respectful and professional when communicating with coworkers. Even if disagreements or misunderstandings exist, avoid taking it personally. Respect the opinions and perspectives of others, and approach conversations with confidence and courtesy.

2. During conversations, pay attention to nonverbal cues to gain a better understanding of how the other person is feeling or what they are thinking about the topic at hand. Remember that your body language can also reveal a great deal about how you feel, so be aware of what it may reveal even when you're not speaking.

3. Speak clearly without rushing through things; this will demonstrate that you have considered your ideas prior to presenting them in a conversation or meeting, thereby demonstrating respect for those present by taking their time into account when communicating effectively.

4. Actively listen to others when they speak by making attentive eye contact, responding appropriately to comments, and asking questions to clarify points of confusion, etc., thereby fostering an open dialogue among all employees as opposed to one-sided conversations occurring only between a few individuals originating from separate corners of the office!

5. Take notes during meetings or conferences to reduce the likelihood of misunderstandings in the future – this could prevent unnecessary back-and-forth between departments for clarification if everything was properly noted down at the time it was initially discussed!

6. Ensure two-way communication – don't just talk over people without giving them a chance to respond - this

can create tension that can lead to further problems in the future, so always keep the lines of communication open regardless of who may hold different opinions than you in the workplace!

7 Finally, keep in mind that feedback should always easily flow in both directions; don't be afraid to provide your managers with constructive criticism when necessary; after all, they are human just like the rest of us and need help understanding our points as well.

Chapter 11: How To Employ Diplomacy To Win Over Your Team

Diplomacy and charisma go hand in hand. To appeal to your team members, clients, and business partners, you must be mindful of what and how you say things. It is common for employees to come from diverse backgrounds and hold diverse perspectives in the workplace. How they interpret what you say is heavily influenced by their personal values and beliefs. As a leader, the last thing you want is to offend someone with your speech due to a lack of tact.

Diplomatic communication involves speaking with empathy and comprehension. You consider the effect of your words, tone of voice, and gestures on the individual or individuals who are listening. The objective is not to persuade those who are listening; rather, it is to be sensitive to their needs and opinions.

Diplomacy is frequently employed in international relations. Diplomats, who represent foreign nations, will serve as intermediaries between nations. Their primary responsibility is to defend their nation's interests without using force or inciting hostility with others. Diplomacy functions in a similar manner in business. It facilitates the development of enduring relationships with internal and external stakeholders. You are able to facilitate discussions and negotiations that result in win-win situations with your team and partners.

You can become a diplomatic communicator by utilising the following three strategies:

Be Careful With Your Words.

Your word selection can affect how others perceive your messages. For example, beginning sentences with "You" can make others feel defensive, whereas beginning sentences with "I" puts them at ease. Consider the following sentences:

You need to just get to work earlier.

I would appreciate it if you arrived earlier to work.

Increasing your vocabulary can also be of great assistance when selecting the appropriate words to convey a message. For instance, telling an employee "The presentation wasn't good" is somewhat deceptive. They may depart pondering, "What did my boss mean by 'not good'?" Possible substitutes for "good" include "engaging," "clear," and "well-researched." Any of these phrases can be used to provide more honest and direct feedback without offending your employees.

Think Before Speaking

Avoid speaking when you are rushed or before you have had adequate time to consider what you want to say. Once uttered, words are irretrievable, like toothpaste squeezed from a tube. What you say can also reveal your leadership skills, so ensure that you've given yourself ample time to deliberate.

It is advisable to avoid making impulsive decisions. Request some time to consider your response and promise to get back to the person shortly. Before speaking during a conversation, pause for a few seconds. This gives the other speaker a few extra seconds to conclude their thoughts, and also gives you time to consider your own position.

Consider Your Nonverbal Signals

Before you even say a word, those who are listening have already formed opinions about what you will say. Imagine entering a boardroom meeting with your shoulders sagging and your head pointed toward the ground. What sort of impact would that have? Or suppose you sat rigidly in your chair with your arms crossed and lips tightly pursed during a teammate's presentation. How relaxed would the presenter be?

Negative body language interferes with verbal communication frequently. You may inadvertently make those around you feel negatively about your message, making it more difficult to influence them and increase employee engagement. Observe yourself in the mirror and try out various positive gestures, facial expressions, and body language. You can also practise relaxing various body parts, such as your facial muscles and shoulders.

Diplomatic communication enables you to take charge of conversations and steer them in a constructive direction for all parties. Your employees will always feel valued after speaking with you, so they may even enjoy the conversation. This can do wonders for your confidence as a leader, as you will be aware that both internal and external stakeholders have faith in you.

Chapter 12: Know Your Audience

Imagine entering a boardroom eager to present a proposal or report you've been working on for three weeks. Your senior managers are gathered in the boardroom, whom you wish to impress.

You take the floor, apprehensive but well-equipped for the task at hand.

As you begin speaking, you observe on people's faces fatigue, boredom, and sarcasm. Perhaps it was the way you were dressed. Or your voice's pitch and tone? The response you have just received from your audience is, "When will this presentation end so I can leave?"

It is common to encounter a hostile crowd. Not everyone will like you or understand your message as you intended. If you look around the boardroom table, auditorium, or classroom, you will see some individuals on their phones, others fidgeting with their ties, and only a few who are attentive and enjoying your message.

Andy Paige, a stylist on the American television network TLC, stated that finding your "one-third" is essential in life. He suggested that regardless of your efforts, one-third of the people you meet will never like you. A further one-third of people will be indifferent to you, neither a fan nor an enemy. However, one-third of individuals are your ardent supporters and will hold favourable opinions of you. Your job is to research and craft your narratives so that they appeal to the one-third and barely attract the remaining two-thirds.

The purpose of public speaking is not to appeal to everyone, but rather to find the one-third of the audience that gets you! How will you identify this individual in a crowded room? It is basic. Your true followers or supporters will be those who make direct contact, demonstrate acknowledgment of what you say, and pose questions or provide constructive feedback.

However, winning over these supporters is difficult. In many instances, particularly when you are addressing a new group of people, they know very little about you. The only difference between them and those who are hostile toward you is that they are receptive to learning and persuasion. Your job is to determine the most effective means of connecting with them and making them feel simply seen and heard.

Abraham Maslow, a renowned psychologist, proposed that after basic needs such as food, shelter, and safety are met, all that humans require is a sense of belonging. A sense of belonging is the feeling of psychological safety within a group of people. When audience members feel a sense of belonging, they feel comfortable being themselves in the presence of the speaker. In return, they demonstrate their gratitude by validating the speaker's message and boosting their confidence on stage.

It is almost as if an unspoken social contract is formed between the speaker and the audience, which goes something like this: If you make me feel accepted, I will support your ideas and message.

Each of these instances exemplifies a homogeneous audience in which all attendees share the same beliefs and objectives. Because your message is likely to resonate with the vast majority of listeners, it is much simpler to address a homogenous audience than a mixed audience. However, there are times when you have no control over who you are speaking to, and you may encounter various types of listeners during your presentations. Knowing the different types of listeners can put you at ease and help you adjust your language, length of speech, humour, and other aspects of your message.

Below is a list of five types of potential listeners:

1. Neutral Listeners

Typically, neutral listeners attend meetings or presentations solely out of obligation. They are either uninterested in the topic or the speaker, or they are sceptical of your message. They are unlikely to indicate interest in your message through facial expressions or body language, so it is never a good idea to use them to gauge the success of your presentation.

2. Uninformed Listeners

Uninformed listeners are typically novices with limited knowledge of the topic of discussion. In contrast to neutral listeners, they are more likely to interact with the speaker when presented with interesting information. Be careful not to lose the attention of uninformed listeners by providing too much information or employing a language that they cannot comprehend.

3. Expert Listeners

Expert listeners are difficult to please because they are extremely knowledgeable about the topic at hand. They are more likely to question the speaker and anticipate new information than to rely on the abundance of information they already possess. Instead of relying on facts and figures to persuade these listeners, offer new perspectives or alternative solutions.

4. Hostile Listeners

Opposing your message or the proposed solutions, hostile listeners have already made up their minds. Instead of being neutral, they are antagonistic. It is extremely challenging to persuade them, but you can at least find common ground and engage in a healthy debate. The advantage of having hostile audience members is that they force you to provide a more balanced argument and seek out the flaws in your perspective. This can greatly assist you in presenting more realistic solutions that consider both advantages and disadvantages.

5. Empathetic Audience

The sympathetic audience is receptive and eager to learn. They are less critical of your message and more likely to identify points with which they agree. Personal anecdotes and emotive language are the most effective ways to keep these types of listeners interested. If your narratives are compelling enough, they will connect with you and become your followers.

Understanding the various types of listeners is the first step. The second step is to learn how to conduct an audience analysis so that you can structure your presentation based on the needs, attitudes, and behaviours of each audience.

Conclusion

Communication is essential in a marriage because it affects the health of the union and the partners' happiness. For a couple to establish a solid family foundation, communication is essential. Communication within a marriage also affects the relationship between family members. A family with effective parent-child communication is happier than one with ineffective parent-parent communication. In a family, effective communication begins with the parents and is imitated by the children. This indicates that communication is essential in a marriage, as its effects can easily extend beyond the couple's relationship and affect the entire family.

The interaction between parents and children will have a significant impact on the manner in which the children are raised.

www.ingramcontent.com/pod-product-compliance
Lightning Source LLC
Chambersburg PA
CBHW050304120526
44590CB00016B/2479